Reading Essentials
in Social Studies

GOVERNING THE WORLD

DEMOCRACY

SUE HURWITZ

Perfection Learning®

To Our Granddaughters
Zimri, Adina, and Olivia
With Love

EDITORIAL DIRECTOR: Susan C. Thies

EDITOR: Judith A. Bates

COVER DESIGN: Michael A. Aspengren

INSIDE DESIGN: Mark Hagenberg, Lori Gould

PHOTO RESEARCH: Lisa Lorimor

IMAGE CREDITS
© Bettmann/CORBIS: p. 7 (top); © Carl & Ann Purcell/CORBIS: p. 38; © CORBIS: p. 35;
© Franklin McMahon/CORBIS: p. 28; © Jose Luis Pelaez, Inc./CORBIS: p. 33;
© Joseph Sohm; ChromoSohm Inc./CORBIS: p. 30; © Owen Franken/CORBIS: p. 39;
© Reuters New Media Inc./CORBIS: p. 44

ArtToday (some images copyright www.arttoday.com) pp. 6, 12,
13, 15, 17, 20, 21, 24, 25, 26, 37 (bottom, right), 43;
Corel: cover (full page), pp. 1, 7 (bottom); Dover Publications: pp. 4, 5, 11;
Library of Congress: back cover, cover (center), pp. 8, 14, 27, 36, 37 (left);
National Archives: cover (top), p. 9, 16, 19; Photodisc: cover (bottom);
Truman Library Collection: pp. 3, 23; United Nations: pp. 41, 42

© 2019 by **Perfection Learning**®

Please visit our Web site at:
www.perfectionlearning.com

When ordering this book, please specify:

Paperback: ISBN 978-0-7891-5907-6 or **38692**
Reinforced Library Binding: ISBN 978-0-7569-4507-7 or **3869202**
eBook: ISBN 978-1-62299-362-8 or **38692D**

Contents

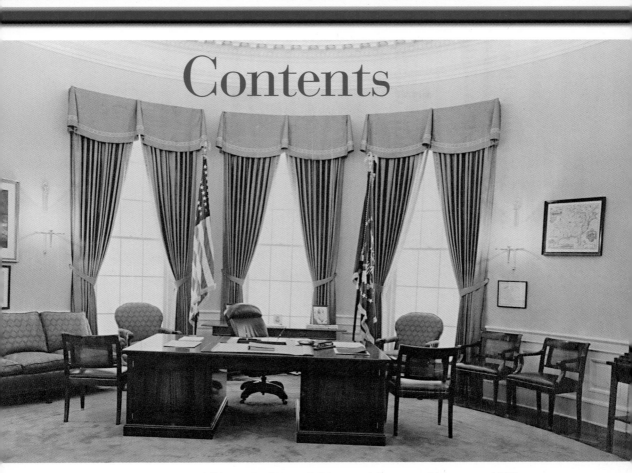

▲ Replica of the Oval Office in the Harry S. Truman Library and Museum, 1977

Introduction

The democratic form of government began in the 6th century B.C. in the Greek **city-state** of Athens. It lasted about 200 years.

The word *democracy* comes from two Greek words—*demo* meaning "people" and *kratos* meaning "rule." Together these words mean "rule by the people."

▲ The political system of ancient Athens (shown above) was a democracy that involved all of its male citizens and not just their representatives. Both decision making and justice were the duty of every citizen.

Only 10 to 15 percent of adults living in ancient Greece had political rights. Women and slaves were not considered citizens, so they had no voting rights. Only male citizens born in Athens could vote.

DIRECT DEMOCRACY

The population of Athens was much smaller than the population in most countries today. So it was easy for *all* male citizens to gather in meetings, or assemblies. They could discuss political issues together and vote directly on how to run their government. This is known as a direct, or pure, democracy.

But a direct democracy is not reasonable today. Populations of most countries are too large to bring everyone together to discuss issues.

REPRESENTATIVE DEMOCRACY

Today, people do not vote directly for many of their laws. They elect other people to vote for them. This representative form of democracy is known as a republic.

The word *republic* comes from two Latin words— *res* meaning "thing" and *publicus* meaning "public."

The republican form of democracy was introduced in Rome. Rome was a region in what is modern-day Italy. The Roman republic began in the 6th century B.C., a short time after democracy began in Athens. The Romans took many of their ideas from the Greeks.

▲ The Forum was the center of Roman civic life for over 500 years. This image, which looks east through the Forum, shows the site during late 19th-century excavations.

The Roman republic expanded far beyond Italy. The republic granted citizenship to the people it conquered. These Roman citizens lived too far from Rome to attend assemblies. So they developed a system of representation. The citizens elected others to represent them at assemblies. These representatives expressed the views of the citizens and voted for them.

In 27 B.C., Rome's republic came to an end. Augustus, the adopted son of Julius Caesar, became the first emperor of the Roman Empire. Emperors ruled the empire for centuries, and they were far from democratic.

SOME DIFFERENCES BETWEEN A DEMOCRACY AND A REPUBLIC

A democracy and a republic are not exactly the same. In a democracy, voters elect representatives. Their representatives must follow the voters' wishes.

In a republic, voters still elect representatives. But their representatives are not obligated to follow their wishes. They may vote for laws that they think are best for the country.

DEMOCRACY IN THE MIDDLE AGES

In 600 A.D., the Vikings in Norway **revived** democratic assemblies. They called their local assemblies Tings.

By 900 A.D., the Vikings expanded their democratic assemblies. They held assemblies in other areas of Scandinavia. Members of the Tings even elected their kings.

The word *ting* is an Old English word meaning a "thing" or an "assembly."

The Vikings were the first to create a supra-Ting, or national assembly. The supra-Ting lasted for centuries. Eventually, the idea spread to England. There the Viking idea of a national assembly **evolved** into the English Parliament.

▶ Drawing from the 1920s showing Viking warriors aboard a drekar, or longship. The Vikings conquered lands to the east and west of Scandinavia.

THE BEGINNING OF MODERN DEMOCRACIES

In 1215 A.D., King John of England was forced to sign the Magna Carta. This document limited the power of the king. It granted some individual freedoms to all people. It also gave them some protection from harsh and unfair treatment by the monarch. The Magna Carta was a major step toward a democratic government.

In the 1600s, people in Western Europe rebelled against their monarchs. Citizens in England and France wanted political and personal freedom. And they wanted to limit the power of their monarchs.

▲ King John signing the Magna Carta, 1215

The idea of a democratic government was brought to America by the Pilgrims. In 1620, they signed the Mayflower Compact before they landed in the colonies. The Mayflower Compact stated that there should be "just and equal laws for all."

◄ The Pilgrims sailed to the New World in 1620 aboard the ship the *Mayflower*. The group hoped to find religious and economic freedom in their new home.

The American Revolution (1775–1783) later expanded the ideas of individual freedom and human rights. As a result, the American colonists broke free from British rule and formed a democratic government.

The United States Declaration of Independence was signed in 1776. It united the 13 colonies in America into a single republic. It established a federal republican form of democracy in the United States. This makes the United States the oldest modern democracy.

When the Declaration of Independence was adopted in 1776, few people in the world were free. This document motivated people around the world to seek freedom.

◄ The reading of the Declaration of Independence from the east balcony of the State House in Boston, 1776

American democracy is based on earlier English and French ideas. The American form of democracy is only about 230 years old. But it has become the role model for other modern democracies.

Even in the 1800s, democracies were different from democracies today. Voting was **restricted** and **corrupt** in many governments. Few personal freedoms were allowed. Many democracies were democracies in name only.

This was still true in the middle of the 20th century. Nations began changing to include democratic **principles** in their **ideals** of governments. But often, these principles were not practiced, and the democracies were actually **dictatorships**.

The democratic form of government is still evolving today. Changes in government are needed as different societies change. For instance, the United States consisted of only 13 states in 1776. Now, there are 50. Democracy in the United States still follows the guidelines of the United States Constitution. But many changes have been made to adjust to the growth of modern America.

▲ The original Declaration of Independence, now exhibited in the Rotunda of the National Archives Building in Washington, D.C., has faded badly—largely because of poor preservation techniques in the 19th century. Today, this priceless document is maintained under the strictest conditions possible.

Chapter 1

The **Democratic** Form of Government

Several forms of government were popular in the ancient world (300 B.C.–500 A.D.) The most common governments were early forms of monarchies. In some cases, tyrannies seized **absolute** power. Oligarchies and aristocracies were others. But there were no democracies until the Greeks of Athens requested a government ruled by many.

Common Forms of Ancient Government

Aristocracy	government based on heredity and ruled by a small group of nobles
Monarchy	government ruled by a king or queen, usually for life and by hereditary right
Oligarchy	government controlled by a small group of people or an organization for its own purposes
Tyranny	government ruled by one or more people who exercise cruel and unjust absolute power

THE FIRST DEMOCRACY

Ancient Greece included many independent city-states. Each city-state had its own government. Athens, an aristocracy, and Sparta, a dictatorship, were the most popular city-states.

Around 570 B.C., Cleisthenes was born to an aristocratic family in Athens. By the time he was 40 years old, he had become a resourceful politician. He had spent time in Sparta and toured other city-states.

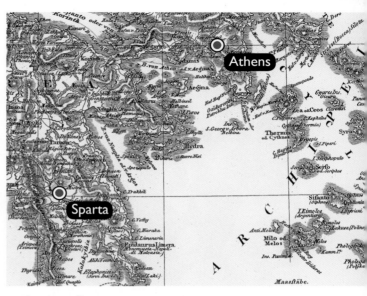

▲ Ancient Greece

Hippias, the nephew of Cleisthenes, was a **brutal** dictator who ruled Athens. In 512 B.C., Cleisthenes asked Sparta for help in overthrowing Hippias. In 510 B.C., Athens was **liberated** from Hippias's rule.

Cleisthenes, who was now in his 60s, hoped to rule Athens. But another aristocrat, Isagoras, challenged Cleisthenes's right to rule.

The aristocrats of Athens supported Isagoras. Cleisthenes promised sweeping government **reforms** and asked the commoners for support. But this time, Sparta helped Isagoras. Isagoras became another tyrant in Athens. Cleisthenes was **exiled**.

In 507 B.C., the commoners of Athens revolted against Isagoras. They exiled Isagoras and seized power for themselves. They recalled Cleisthenes from exile.

The commoners viewed dictatorship as the worst possible form of government. They wanted something different.

They asked Cleisthenes to create a new government that included the commoners. This was an entirely new idea. Previously, only aristocrats had been included in Greek governments.

Cleisthenes created the form of government that we now know as a democracy. The democracy of Cleisthenes included both commoners and aristocrats.

▲ Pericles, grandnephew of Cleisthenes, delivers a persuasive speech to a crowd in ancient Greece.

In 507 B.C., the democratic form of government in Athens became the world's first government ruled by many.

Between 461 B.C. until his death in 429 B.C., Pericles became a great Athenian leader. The Assembly became the central power of Athens. The Assembly consisted of only male citizens. Women and slaves were still denied citizenship. The rules of citizenship were narrowed even more to include only males born of two Athenian parents. Athenian democracy was not perfect, but it was close. And it worked.

This period in Greek history became known as the Golden Age, or the Age of Pericles. The city of Athens became the center of some of the greatest architecture, art, philosphy, and literature in the history of the world.

The Golden Age ended in 404 B.C. when Athens was defeated by Sparta.

THE IMPORTANCE OF GREEK AND ROMAN DEMOCRACIES

The democracies of the ancient Greeks and Romans were entirely new forms of government. Centuries later, these two ancient democracies influenced the founders of American democracy. Modern democracies have based many of their political theories of government on these two ancient civilizations.

John Locke

THE GROWTH OF DEMOCRACY

During the Middle Ages, Christian teachings stated that all men were created equal in the eyes of God. Such teachings helped spread the idea of equality.

John Locke was an English **philosopher**. In 1690, he published a book entitled *Two Treatises.* Locke stated that a government's job was to protect the "natural rights" of people. These natural rights included "the right to life, liberty, and the ownership of property."

In 1762, Jean Jacques Rousseau, a French philosopher, wrote the book *The Social Contract.*

Jean Jacques Rousseau

Thomas Jefferson

In it, Rousseau further developed the ideas of John Locke. He said that the ideas of the people should be included in how their government is run.

American statesmen Thomas Jefferson and James Madison refined the philosophies of Locke and Rousseau. The two Americans used the philosophers' ideas in the American Declaration of Independence (1776) and the United States Constitution (1787).

During the 1800s, settlers moved into the American frontier. Because of the harsh living conditions, the settlers depended on cooperation and sharing. This helped break down class differences and **prejudices**. In this way, the American pioneers gained respect for the individual rights of one another.

By the end of the 19th century, major Western European monarchies were becoming less powerful. The **commoners** fought for and won the right of more voice in their governments. The early British Parliament became a popular example for global democracies.

By the middle of the 20th century, most countries in the world included some democratic ideals in their governments. But the practice of democracy was often in name only.

James Madison

Chapter 2

Modern **Democracy** Begins in America

▲ President Abraham Lincoln delivering the Gettysburg Address on November 19, 1863

. . . that government of the people, by the people, and for the people, shall not perish from this earth.

This definition of democracy is from the Gettysburg Address given by President Abraham Lincoln in 1863. Democracies are more than just forms of government. Democracies are based on certain ideals or principles and guarantee their citizens a certain way of life.

Not all democracies have their principles written down. These democracies are based on customs, common law, and **statutes**. But most democracies today do have written constitutions. These governments are called *constitutional democracies*. Constitutional democracies limit the power of their governments and the officials who run them.

CONSTITUTIONS

A constitution is a written document that explains the law of the land. It is a plan of how the government will work. A constitution establishes the authority of the democracy and defines the limits and duties of the government.

CREATING THE UNITED STATES CONSTITUTION

Constitutions must be capable of change. The United States has the world's oldest written democratic constitution. The Constitution has 7 brief articles and 27 amendments.

The amendments keep the Constitution up-to-date. Without them, the United States Constitution could not have survived unchanged until today.

> The articles of the Constitution are the parts that deal with a particular subject. Amendments are additions to the original Constitution.

THE ARTICLES OF CONFEDERATION

In 1777, the new states in America adopted an agreement called the Articles of **Confederation**. During the American Revolution, which was fought between the colonies and England, the Continental Congress used this document as a guide for the new government.

Under the Articles of Confederation, the new states were loosely united in a confederation. Each state still remained independent, or **sovereign**.

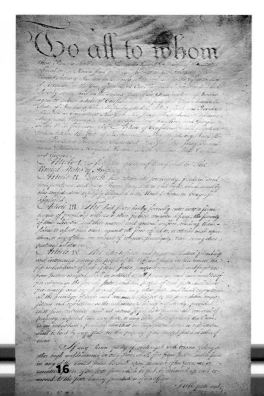

◄ The Articles of Confederation served as the basic law of the land until 1789 when the United States Constitution was adopted.

The Articles of Confederation were only partially successful because the document could not require the states to do anything, either individually or together. The confederation was too weak to unite the independent states under one government.

▲ Constitutional Convention, 1787

James Madison played a very important role at the Constitutional Convention. Many of his valuable ideas were included in the Constitution. He later wrote the first **draft** of the Bill of Rights and worked to get it accepted. Although he was a short, shy man, he was a giant of a politician. He later became the fourth president of the United States.

THE CONSTITUTIONAL CONVENTION

In 1787, 55 state **delegates** met in Philadelphia to draw up a constitution. These men were appointed by the **legislatures** of the different states. George Washington, a delegate from Virginia, was **unanimously** elected president of the convention.

The delegates included men who were lawyers, soldiers, and **planters**. Most of them were **statesmen** and politicians who were experienced in the history of government. They had studied Greek and Roman democracies. They were familiar with the British Parliament.

At the time of the Constitutional Convention, the former 13 colonies were afraid of forming a strong national government. They wanted to avoid a monarchy like the one in England. The 13 new states also had a great variety of needs. These differing needs caused some difficulty when the delegates tried to agree on sections of the Constitution.

Some Constitutional Concerns of the States

By the time the Constitutional Convention met, the delegates were ready to make some **compromises**. They realized that the states had to give up certain powers to make a strong national government. Yet the delegates to the convention still were extremely loyal to their states.

One of the major conflicts at the convention was between the larger states and the smaller states. Each state was concerned about how it would be represented in a lawmaking body. Would the number of votes available to each state be based on

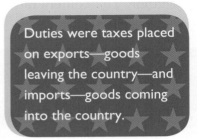

Duties were taxes placed on exports—goods leaving the country—and imports—goods coming into the country.

population or size? Or would the states have equal votes? Other concerns included **territorial** rights, and the issues of slavery, religion, and export and import duties.

The Connecticut Compromise

The Constitutional Convention devised a compromise when they created the United States Congress. The Convention satisfied the concerns of both the smaller states and the larger states.

The convention established a **bicameral**, or two-house, legislature. Together the houses, the House of Representatives and the Senate, are called Congress.

Today, the Senate is made up of two senators from each state—100 members in all. Members in the House of Representatives are determined by each state's population. States with large populations, such as California, may have more than 50 representatives. States with small populations, such as Alaska, may only have 1.

State population figures may vary when a **census** recounts the population of each state. But no matter how small a state's population becomes, it always will have at least one member in the House. In 2002, the House was made up of 435 members.

Completion of the United States Constitution

The delegates at the Constitutional Convention eventually settled their differences. After nearly four months, they completed the Constitution. It was signed on September 17, 1787.

The Constitution has been proclaimed a great achievement. But today, few Americans know much about it.

What rights and freedoms are included in the United States Constitution? What is the Bill of Rights?

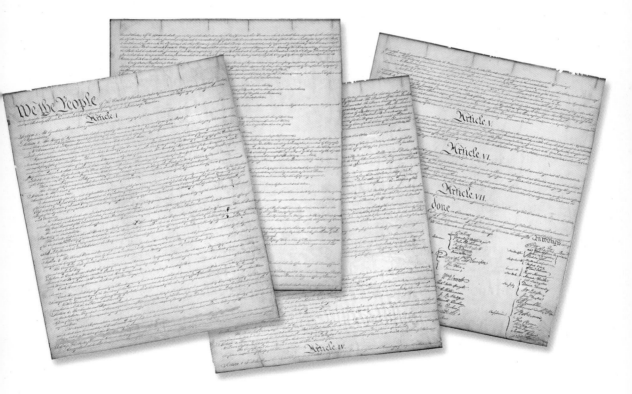

▲ United States Constitution

Chapter 3

The **United States** Constitution

We the People of the United States, in Order to form a more perfect Union, establish Justice, insure domestic Tranquility, provide for the common defense, promote the general Welfare, and secure the Blessings of Liberty to ourselves and our Posterity, do ordain and establish this Constitution for the United States of America.

The preamble, or introduction, to the United States Constitution is stated above. It sets six goals for the United States Constitution.

- to form a more perfect Union (a better government)
- to establish Justice (fairness in the way people are treated and decisions are made)
- to insure domestic Tranquility (peace in the United States)
- to provide for the common defense (the protection of everyone)
- to promote the general Welfare (the physical, social, and financial conditions)
- to secure the Blessings of Liberty to ourselves and to our Posterity (freedom for current citizens and future generations)

The following is an abridged, or shortened, version of the first three articles of the United States Constitution. These articles establish the three branches of the federal government. They are the legislative, the executive, and the judicial branches.

The three branches of the federal government create a system of **checks** and **balances**. Each branch is separate and has its own power and responsibilities. Yet each acts to check the power of the other two branches.

The founding fathers created the system of checks and balances so that one branch would not become more powerful than the others. For example, the president can veto, or turn down, a bill that Congress passes. In turn, with enough votes, Congress can overturn a veto.

ARTICLE I
THE LEGISLATIVE BRANCH

Section 1

- *All Legislative Powers herein granted shall be vested in a Congress of the United States, which shall consist of a Senate and a House of Representatives.*

Section 2

- *The House of Representatives shall be composed of Members chosen every second Year by the People of the several States . . .*
- *The House of Representatives shall choose their Speaker and other Officers; and shall have the sole Power of **Impeachment**.*

▲ Construction began on the United States Capitol Building in 1793. Today, it contains 540 rooms and houses the legislative branch of government.

Section 3

- *The Senate of the United States shall be composed of two Senators from each State for six Years; and each Senator shall have one Vote.*
- *The Vice President of the United States shall be President of the Senate, but shall have no Vote, unless they be equally divided.*

Section 7

- *All Bills for raising Revenue shall originate in the House of Representatives; but the Senate may propose or concur with Amendments as on other Bills.*

The idea that tax bills originate in the House comes from British Parliament where tax bills originated in the House of Commons. It was thought that the representatives in the House of Commons knew better what the people wanted. But in the United States, the Senate can amend tax bills. Britain's House of Lords cannot.

Section 8

- *The Congress shall have Power To lay and collect Taxes, Duties, Imposts and Excises, to pay the Debts and provide for the common Defense and general Welfare of the United States . . .*

Duties, imposts, and excises are all forms of taxes. Duties are taxes on imports and exports. Imposts are taxes on goods brought into a country. Excises are taxes on goods intended for the home market.

Among other powers, Section 8 provides for the United States to borrow and to coin money and to establish post offices. Congress also has the power to declare war and to raise and support armies and a navy.

Powers forbidden to Congress are addressed in Section 9. Those forbidden to the states are in Section 10.

▲ The White House was completed in 1800 and has been the home of every president since John Adams. The executive branch of government conducts its business from the Oval Office located in the White House.

ARTICLE II
THE EXECUTIVE BRANCH

Section 1

- *The executive Power shall be vested in a President of the United States of America. He shall hold his Office during the Term of four Years, and, together with the Vice President, chosen for the same Term . . .*

Among other powers, each state may appoint the number of electors equal to the number of senators and representatives that the state has in Congress. These electors will vote for their state in electing the United States president and vice president.

Ballots from the electors will be counted by the president of the Senate. The candidate having the greatest number of votes will become president. In case of a tie vote, the House of Representatives will choose one candidate to become president.

- *Before he enters on the Execution of his Office, he shall take the following Oath or Affirmation;—"I do solemnly swear (or affirm) that I will faithfully execute the Office of the President of the United States, and will to the best of my Ability, preserve, protect, and defend the Constitution of the United States."*

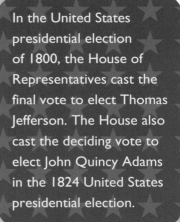

In the United States presidential election of 1800, the House of Representatives cast the final vote to elect Thomas Jefferson. The House also cast the deciding vote to elect John Quincy Adams in the 1824 United States presidential election.

◄ The inauguration of George Washington on the balcony of the City Hall in New York City, 1789

▲ On December 8, 1941, the day after the bombing at Pearl Harbor, President Franklin D. Roosevelt appeared before Congress and requested a declaration of war against Japan.

Section 2

- *The President shall be Commander in Chief of the Army and Navy of the United States, and of the **Militia** of the several States, when called into the actual service of the United States . . .*

As commander in chief, the president may ask for reports from the military branches of the United States. Among other powers in Section 2, the president may grant pardons for offenses against the United States, except in cases of impeachment.

On August 9, 1974, former President Richard Nixon resigned because of his involvement in the Watergate Scandal. On September 8, 1974, President Gerald R. Ford used the power in Article II, Section 2 to pardon Nixon for any illegal acts that he might have committed while president, thus eliminating the possibility of criminal proceedings against the former president.

Calvin Coolidge

Section 3

- *He shall from time to time give to the Congress Information of the State of the Union . . .*

The president of the United States gives a yearly speech about how our union, or country, is progressing. The president gives this annual message, called the State of the Union Address, in person to Congress.

President Calvin Coolidge's 1923 speech was the first to be broadcast on radio. President Harry Truman's State of the Union Address was the first to be broadcast on television.

Earlier in our history, United States presidents delivered this message to Congress. Citizens of the United States learned the contents of the address later when it was published in newspapers and magazines. After the arrival of radio and television, the State of the Union message was shared with the American people at the same time it was given to Congress.

Harry S. Truman

▲ Until 1935, the Supreme Court had no permanent home. From 1819 to 1860, it met in the chamber above, which has been restored in the Capitol Building. Today, the Court meets in the Supreme Court Building.

The Supreme Court is comprised of nine members—the chief justice and eight associate justices. The justices are appointed by the president and confirmed by Congress.

ARTICLE III
THE JUDICIAL BRANCH

Section 1

- *The Judicial Power of the United States, shall be vested in one supreme Court, and in such inferior Courts as the Congress may from time to time ordain and establish. . . .*

The Supreme Court is the highest court in the land. State courts are referred to as inferior courts because they have less authority than the Supreme Court. Justices of the Supreme Court decide whether laws **comply** with the United States Constitution.

◄ *Boy on Trial,* a drawing by Franklin McMahon

Section 2

- *The Trial of All Crimes, except in Cases of Impeachment, shall be by Jury . . .*

By custom, 12 people make up a jury. But neither the Constitution nor the Bill of Rights lists a specific number. A jury should represent people from a wide variety of backgrounds.

In 1946, the Supreme Court ruled that no person can be excluded from serving on a jury because of race, religion, beliefs, or income.

Section 3

- ***Treason*** *against the United States shall consist only in levying War against them, or in adhering to their Enemies, giving them Aid and Comfort. No Person shall be convicted of Treason unless on the Testimony of two Witnesses to the same **overt** Act, or on Confession in open Court.*

THE SUPREME LAW OF THE LAND

Although the United States Constitution was written in 1787, it did not go into effect until 1788. It became the "supreme law of the land" on June 21, 1788, when New Hampshire became the ninth state to **ratify** it. In early January the ratifying states selected presidential electors, and on February 4, 1789, they named George Washington the first president.

The United States
Bill of Rights

Many felt that the United States Constitution gave too much power to the federal, or national, government. The Bill of Rights consists of the first ten amendments to the United States Constitution. They were added in 1791, after the Constitution was formally approved.

The United States Bill of Rights protects the basic rights and freedoms of individuals. It lists certain natural rights every United States citizen is born with. These include personal and political freedoms.

The following is a list of the individual freedoms and rights guaranteed by the United States Bill of Rights.

THE FIRST AMENDMENT
Freedom of Religion, Speech, and the Press
Right to Assemble

*Congress shall make no law respecting an establishment of religion, or prohibiting the free exercise thereof; or abridging the freedom of speech, or of the press; or the right of people to peaceably assemble, and to petition the Government for a **redress** of grievances.*

The First Amendment protects the right of religious freedom and promotes religious **tolerance** of others. It protects freedom of speech and freedom of the press. It also protects the right of people to gather, or to assemble.

In the United States, reporters are not penalized for relating facts. They can even point out the governments' shortcomings. The right of free press, while a principle of a democracy, is not always allowed in other forms of government. In recent years, some United States reporters in foreign countries have lost their lives for their honest reports.

▲ Under the First Amendment, these citizens had the right to hold a protest in 1985 against the nuclear arms race.

Citizens must be free to assemble in special groups. Political parties and organizations are examples of such groups. A democracy allows thousands of these private groups. The existence of such a variety of ethnic, religious, and political groups is called *pluralism*.

Some private organizations support candidates for public office. Others debate political issues. Still others try to influence political policy decisions. Some try to educate citizens about voting issues.

Democracies do not interfere with private organizations. Some forms of government *do* interfere with private organizations. They harass people who attend such groups. Other governments do not permit private organizations at all. Two examples of such governments are dictatorships and communist governments.

THE SECOND AMENDMENT
Right to Bear Arms

A well-regulated Militia, being necessary to the security of a free State, the right of the people to keep and bear Arms, shall not be infringed.

The Second Amendment guarantees the right to own guns for personal protection. Today, this has become a **controversial** amendment. Due to an increase in random killings, Congress is considering stricter gun-control laws. State legislators are pushing for gun-control laws that are even stricter than those recommended by Congress.

The United States is one of few nations where gun possession is so widespread. In the United Kingdom, even the police do not carry guns. Still, the United Kingdom is supporting stricter gun controls. Brazil, Cambodia, and China also are moving toward more strict gun control.

THE THIRD AMENDMENT
Housing Soldiers

No soldier shall, in time of peace be quartered in any house, without the consent of the Owner, nor in time of war, but in a manner to be prescribed by law.

American colonists had been obligated to keep British soldiers in their homes against their will. James Madison included this amendment to make sure that Americans would never need to do so again.

THE FOURTH AMENDMENT
Search Warrants

*The right of the people to be secure in their persons, houses, papers, and effects, against unreasonable searches and seizures, shall not be violated, and no **Warrants** shall issue, but upon probable cause, supported by Oath or affirmation, and particularly describing the place to be searched, and the persons or things to be seized.*

The Fourth Amendment protects citizens from prosecution based on evidence obtained by a search without a warrant. Law officials are required in most cases to obtain a search or arrest warrant from a judge. Some instances, such as a search at an airport to protect national security, would not require a search warrant.

THE FIFTH AMENDMENT
Rights in Criminal Cases

*No person shall be held to answer for a capital, or otherwise infamous crime, unless on a presentment or **indictment** of a Grand Jury, except in cases arising in the land or naval forces, or in the Militia, when actual service in time of War or public danger; nor shall any person be subject for the same offense to be twice put in jeopardy of life or limb; nor shall be compelled in any criminal case to be a witness against himself, nor be deprived of life, liberty, or property, without due process of law; nor shall private property be taken for public use, without just compensation.*

Capital crimes are unlawful acts that are punishable by death. Infamous crimes are those that are punishable by either death or imprisonment.

The Fifth Amendment protects the right to remain silent. It keeps a person from **incriminating** himself or herself. When people use this right, they are "taking the Fifth."

The Fifth Amendment also protects people from standing trial more than once for the same charges. That would be **double jeopardy**.

THE SIXTH AMENDMENT
Right to a Fair Trial

*In all criminal prosecutions, the accused shall enjoy the right to a speedy and public trial, by an impartial jury of the State and district wherein the crime shall have been committed . . . and to be informed of the nature and cause of the accusation; to be confronted with the witnesses against him; to have **compulsory** process for obtaining witnesses in his favor, and to have the Assistance of Counsel for his defense.*

A person accused of a crime is guaranteed a public trial within a reasonable amount of time. He or she must be informed of the charges and granted the assistance of a lawyer.

Juries usually are selected from a random list of names obtained from registered voters or people with driver's licenses. A jury usually consists of 12 members of the community and peers of the accused.

THE SEVENTH AMENDMENT
Rights in Civil Cases

In suits at common law, where the value in controversy shall exceed twenty dollars, the right of trial by jury shall be preserved, and no fact tried by jury shall be otherwise reexamined in any Court of the United States, than according to the rules of the common law.

In 1791, $20 was equivalent to about 40 days' pay. Today, the amount of money required in federal civil cases must be greater than $10,000. Lawsuits between citizens of different states must exceed $50,000.

Common law relates to the customary practices created by past judicial decisions. Civil law refers to the disputes of citizens among themselves.

THE EIGHTH AMENDMENT
Bails, Fines, and Punishments

*Excessive **bail** shall not be required, nor excessive fines imposed, nor cruel and unusual punishments inflicted.*

A jail sentence is the usual punishment for most crimes in the United States. People lose their liberties when they are confined in jail.

In some states and for some federal crimes, death is the punishment. But this has been an issue in the courts for many years. Some people feel this is cruel and unusual punishment.

THE NINTH AMENDMENT
Rights of Citizens

The enumeration in the Constitution, of certain rights, shall not be construed to deny or disparage others retained by the people.

The Ninth Amendment guarantees that any rights not listed in the first eight amendments belong to the people, not the government. This might include the right to vote, or the right to be considered innocent until proven guilty.

THE TENTH AMENDMENT
Rights of States and Citizens

The powers not delegated to the United States by the Constitution, nor prohibited by it to the States, are reserved to the States respectively, or to the people.

The Tenth Amendment limits the power of the federal government to issues already written down. Other powers belong to the states and the citizens.

THE IMPORTANCE OF THE BILL OF RIGHTS

Former United States President Harry S. Truman summed up the importance of the Bill of Rights. He said, "The Bill of Rights, contained in the first ten amendments of the Constitution, is every American's guarantee of freedom."

Chapter 5

Additional
Amendments

So far, Amendments 11 to 27 have been added to the United States Constitution. These are not listed or considered part of the United States Bill of Rights although they guarantee additional rights.

SLAVERY

For the majority of its first 100 years, the United States struggled with the issue of slavery. In December of 1865, the 13th Amendment to the Constitution was ratified, ending slavery.

▲ An engraving from the 1860s celebrating the emancipation of slaves

PROHIBITION OF LIQUOR

The 18th Amendment, ratified in 1920, made it illegal to make, sell, or transport liquor. This is the only amendment to be repealed, or withdrawn. In 1933, the 21st Amendment overturned the 18th. It was again lawful to make, sell, and transport liquor in states that did not have their own prohibition laws.

LIMITATION OF PRESIDENTS TO TWO TERMS

In 1932, Franklin D. Roosevelt was elected president of the United States. He was elected again in 1936, 1940, and 1944. He became the first president to serve four terms in office.

Many people felt that four terms were too long for one man to serve as president. So in 1951, the 22nd Amendment was ratified. It limits the president to serving only two elected terms.

▲ Women sponsored rallies and parades in the late 1800s and early 1900s to promote voting rights for women.

VOTING RIGHTS AND FAIR ELECTIONS

The right to vote is guaranteed in the United States Constitution. In the United States today, every citizen who is at least 18 years of age has the right to vote in general government elections. But these voting rights were not always the same.

The United States Declaration of Independence states that all men are created equal. Yet African American men did not receive voting rights until the 15th Amendment to the United States Constitution passed in 1870. And despite the freedoms guaranteed in the 15th Amendment, the voting rights of African Americans were restricted until the 1970s. These restrictions were removed as a result of civil rights laws.

Suffrage is a basic right in democracies. But suffrage often evolves slowly. The participation and peaceful demonstrations of citizens may bring about important changes in government. American women did not receive the right to vote until the 19th Amendment to the Constitution was passed in 1920.

And in 1971, the 26th Amendment granted the right to vote to all citizens who are 18 years and older.

The right to vote includes responsibilities. One major responsibility is to know the issues being voted upon. A voter must learn as much as possible about the facts of each issue.

Another responsibility of a voter is to get out and vote. For a long time, people have struggled for the right to vote. But today, a large number of people do not take advantage of this right.

Switzerland, another long-term democracy, did not grant its female citizens voting rights in national elections until 1971.

In a representative democracy such as the United States, it is important that people vote for their representatives. People must be active in influencing and controlling the political process. People do this with their votes!

▲ Campaign for suffrage days in New Jersey in the early 1900s

Chapter 6

Other Forms of **Democracy**

In democratic governments, citizens vote in free and competitive elections. Citizens also have civil liberties such as freedom of speech, religion, press, and assembly. Forms of governments that include these freedoms may vary and still be considered democratic.

PARLIAMENTARY DEMOCRACIES

A parliament is a branch of a national government. It is similar to the United States Congress. Both the United States Congress and a parliament are lawmaking branches of government.

Some countries in the Caribbean, such as Aruba and Jamaica, have parliamentary democracies. In parliamentary democracies, the chief executive is chosen by and responsible to the parliament. That person is a prime minister. Among other titles are premier, chancellor, or minister-president.

▲ Parliament Building, Tokyo, Japan

PARLIAMENTARY DEMOCRACIES RECOGNIZING A MONARCH

Japan has a parliamentary democracy that recognizes a monarch. Other countries that have a democracy blended with a monarchy are Greenland, Belize, Spain, and Belgium.

FEDERAL REPUBLICS

The United States has a federal republic form of government. Modern federal republics first began with the United States. Other federal republics include France, much of Latin America, and the Philippines. Mexico, Brazil, India, and Switzerland also have federal republic forms of democracy.

In federal republics, the chief executives are presidents elected by the voters. The presidents are responsible to the voters, not to Congress.

Federal republics have two levels of government. They have a federal, or national, level and a state level. The federal government focuses on what is best for the country. State governments focus on what is best for each state.

◄ The National Assembly of France meets in its chambers in Paris.

CONFEDERATIONS

A confederate democracy is similar to a federal system. But a confederation gives less power to the national government. A confederation is made up of independent states. These states join together to form one government.

Each state in a confederation has absolute control over its citizens and territory. Laws of the central government concern the states, provinces, or territories.

For example, some people in Canada live in the province of Quebec. They must follow laws made in Quebec. They also must follow laws made by the Canadian government.

During the American Revolution, the colonies set up a confederation. They stated their principles in the Articles of Confederation. But this form of government gave the states too much power. That made the confederation weak.

Later the colonists decided to form a federation. This federal democratic form of government was included in the United States Constitution.

The main difference between confederations and federal republics is in the balance of power. A confederation gives more power to the states. A federal republic gives less power to the states.

Confederations are not common today. A confederation government is not as strong as a federal government. In a confederation, members may withdraw at any time.

THE SPREAD OF MODERN DEMOCRACY

In 1790, there were only three nations with democratic governments. They were the United States, Switzerland, and France.

By the 1950s, most independent nations around the world had governments that included some democratic ideals. By 1990, there were 61 democracies worldwide. Today, more than 125 countries have some form of democracy.

The successful democracy of the United States has influenced other countries during the past 200 years. The popularity of the democratic form of government also has been spread by the United Nations.

▲ Lights float above the activities of the Security Council. The most momentous decisions of the UN are made by this group of delegates. In the background is a mural depicting man in struggle and in triumph.

THE UNITED NATIONS

The United Nations was founded in 1945 when World War II ended. Nations from all over the world are members. The UN is dedicated to maintaining world peace.

The United Nations believes that people can govern themselves, which is the democratic form of government. The UN promotes the idea that people are born with certain human rights.

In 1948, the United Nations issued a Universal Declaration of Human Rights. This document is as important as the American Bill of Rights and the British Magna Carta.

The Universal Declaration has done much in educating nations in developing democratic ideals. The United Nations also has influenced nations to grant their citizens more rights and freedoms.

The preamble to the 1948 Universal Declaration of Human Rights of the United Nations reads as follows.

Whereas the peoples of the United Nations have in the Charter reaffirmed their faith in fundamental human rights, in the dignity and worth of the human person, and in the equal rights of men and women and have determined to promote the social progress and better standards of life in larger freedom.

Following the preamble, 30 articles stress freedoms and rights similar to those found in the United States Bill of Rights.

The Universal Declaration is not a law, and it is not legally binding. But it has had a positive moral impact on nations around the world.

The principles stated in the declaration, like the United States Bill of Rights, are the very core of the democratic form of government.

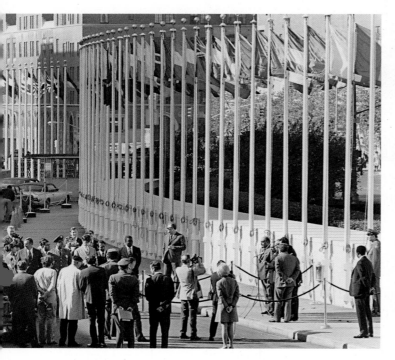

▲ As with most long-established institutions, the UN has its moments of ceremony. The ceremony shown above is the traditional flag-raising ritual performed to initiate new member countries into the fraternity of nations.

Conclusion

The democracies that began in ancient Athens and Rome were models for American democracy. American democracy, in turn, has become a model for the democracies of other nations.

The United States Constitution has served America well. That American democracy has thrived for more than 200 years has not been by accident. American democracy is constantly evolving. Constitutional amendments have kept the United States Constitution **flexible**. They have allowed the United States to meet the needs of a growing nation.

Another factor in the success of American democracy has been free public education. Democracies, ruled by the people, depend on well-educated voters. People cannot vote wisely if they do not understand voting issues.

The practice of democracy must be learned. Americans are guaranteed 12 years of free public education. This education goes a long way in safeguarding the needs of democracy. Any person who "drops out of school" before completing his or her education is weakening American democracy.

Thirty-four international wars were fought between 1945 and 1989. None of the wars were between modern representative democracies. Democratic countries have fought wars with nondemocratic countries. But representative democracies have not fought wars with one another.

▲ Independence Hall in Philadelphia, Pennsylvania, is often called "the birthplace of the United States." Within its walls, the Declaration of Independence was adopted, the Continental Congress wrote the Articles of Confederation, and the Federal Constitutional Convention drafted the United States Constitution.

Representative democracies share similar ideals. They try to peaceably work out any differences that may occur. Democracies all over the world support one another. That support is obvious when conflicts arise among nations around the world today.

Today, the democratic form of government is still spreading among nations. North and South America are continents in which democracies flourish. Africa has some recently formed democracies. Asian countries, such as South Korea, have experienced a growth of democracies. Some former Soviet Union republics are creating democratic governments.

As long as people insist on individual freedoms and rights, democracies should thrive. The future of the democratic form of government seems healthy and secure.

▲ Soldiers of Ukraine's Presidential Regiment look through ballot papers at a polling station in Kiev, March 31, 2002.

Internet Connections
to Democracy

http://www.encyclopedia.com
Search this kid-friendly encyclopedia for topics relating to democracy, the Constitution, and the Declaration of Independence. Then click on the many links to further your knowledge.

http://www.infoplease.com/ce6/history/A0815129.html
Information is provided about democracy and its development.

https://www.cia.gov/library/publications/the-world-factbook/
The World Factbook is a publication created from intelligence gathered by the United States Central Intelligence Agency. It contains maps and profiles of every country in the world, including information about the type of government each country has.

http://www.historyforkids.org/learn/government/democracy.htm
This site has information about democracies in ancient times.

http://www.historyforkids.org/learn/greeks/history/classical.htm
Learn about Cleisthenes who invented the democratic form of government.

http://www.un.org/Overview/rights.html
View the Universal Declaration of Human Rights adopted by the United Nations in 1948.

Glossary

absolute having total power or authority

bail sum of money deposited to secure an accused person's temporary release from custody. It guarantees that person's appearance in court at a later date

balance something that offsets or counters the influence of something else

bicameral having two separate and distinct lawmaking assemblies

brutal harsh and cruel

census official count of a population carried out at set intervals

check means of controlling or restraining someone or something

city-state independent state consisting of a sovereign (see separate entry) city and its surrounding territory

commoner ordinary member of society who does not belong to the nobility

comply obey or conform to something, such as a rule, law, or regulation

compromise settlement of a dispute in which two or more sides agree to accept less than they originally wanted

compulsory required by law

confederation group of states that form a political unit in which they keep most of their independence but act together for certain purposes such as defense

controversial having a strong disagreement

corrupt immoral or dishonest

delegate someone chosen to represent or to act for another person or group

dictatorship government whose leader rules with absolute (see separate entry) power and force

double jeopardy prosecution of someone a second time for something that he or she has already been tried for

draft rough version of something written

evolve to develop gradually

exile to order someone to leave and stay away from his or her home country as a punishment

flexible able to change according to circumstances

ideal standard or principle (see separate entry) which people use as a goal

impeachment act of charging a government official with serious misconduct while in office

incriminate to provide evidence of someone's guilt

indictment formal accusation of a serious crime

legislature official body with the power to make, change, and repeal laws

liberate to release from political or military control

militia army of soldiers who are civilians but take military training and serve full-time in emergencies

overt done openly without any attempt to conceal the action

philosopher person who studies basic concepts such as truth, existence, reality, and freedom

planter someone who owns or manages a large estate or farm

prejudice hatred, fear, or mistrust of a person or group, especially one of a particular religion, ethnicity, nationality, or social status

principle basic way in which something works

ratify to give formal approval to something, usually an agreement, in order for it to become valid or operative

redress means or possibility of correcting something

reform particular change or improvement

restricted limited

revive to bring something back

sovereign self-governing and not ruled by any other state

statesman senior politician widely respected for high standards and concern for the public good

statute law

suffrage right to vote

territorial relating to land or water owned or claimed

tolerance acceptance of differing views

treason violation of the loyalty by a person to his or her country

unanimously with all members in agreement with one another

warrant document that gives law enforcement particular rights or powers, such as the right to search or arrest someone

Index